MEDITERRANEAN MEALS

25 Delicious Recipes and the 7 Sicilian Superfoods to Lose Weight and Stay Healthy for Life

By

Angelo Acquista, M.D.

Author of the #1 Bestselling Mediterranean diet book,

The Mediterranean Prescription

Please note: No book can replace the diagnostic expertise and medical advice of a trusted physician. Please be sure to consult with your doctor before making any decisions that affect your health, particularly if you suffer from any medical condition or have any symptom that may require treatment.

To my wife, Svetlana, and children, Alessandra, Nicky and Sally,
for letting me try many versions of my recipes on them first.

Introduction

Born in Castrofilippo, Sicily, where he lived until the age of nine, Dr. Angelo Acquista knows from his own experience why, as he jokes, "Sicilians are so healthy and long-lived you have to shoot them to kill them." As a medical doctor he is well aware of the latest scientific studies showing how the Mediterranean foods that Sicilians eat every day can promote weight loss, help extend and improve the quality of life, and protect against diseases ranging from a variety of cancers, to immune and metabolic disorders, to coronary and vascular diseases.

Italian food is inarguably one of the most popular cuisines in the world, but the ingredients and cuisines of Italy differ significantly from one region to another. Northern Italian cooking generally uses butter rather than olive oil, more wine and broth than tomatoes or tomato sauce, and more polenta and risotto than pasta. In Central Italy you will find many dishes using grilled or roasted meats. Northern and Central Italy also tend to favor stuffed pastas made with eggs while the South is generally known for its dry pasta. The farther south you go, the longer and hotter the growing season, so more olive oil is used, along with more tomatoes, fish, and vegetables. Based on the scientific and medical evidence, Sicilian cuisine is undoubtedly the healthiest of them all.

Sicily, the largest island in the Mediterranean, is located just off the southern tip of the toe of the Italian boot. The abundant fresh fruits, vegetables, and nuts, as well as the extra-virgin olive oil and fresh-caught fish that form the basis of the traditional Sicilian diet, have earned it the well-deserved nickname "God's kitchen."

The Mediterranean meals that follow are created around 7 specific Sicilian "Superfoods":

- Olive oil
- Cruciferous vegetables
- Tomatoes
- Nuts
- Berries
- Legumes
- Fish

These are the foods that make Sicilian cuisine not only the most effective of all the versions of the Mediterranean diet, but also one of the healthiest diets in the world. This is not opinion, but rather the conclusion of decades of scientific research.

In the last couple of years there have been substantial and persuasive new studies showing that these foods have significant and far-reaching benefits for our health and wellness. One study, for example, conducted at the University of Cordoba in Spain and published in *BMC Genomics*, shows that specific components in extra-virgin olive oil may suppress genes that promote inflammation on the cellular level, which is known to be a precursor of heart disease and diabetes. Among the many other studies cited here, one shows that eating tree nuts (which include almonds, cashews, chestnuts, hazelnuts, pine nuts, and walnuts, among others) can reduce the risk of coronary artery disease and can also encourage weight loss. Another study, based on information gathered from 90,630 women participating in the Nurses Health Study II, found that eating beans or lentils (i.e., legumes) two or more times a week was associated with a 24 percent reduced risk of breast cancer.

Eating all these foods prepared in the traditional Sicilian manner—which means grilling, broiling, baking, and boiling rather than frying—also promotes natural weight loss. In addition to explaining the significance of all the research supporting the many health benefits of the 7 Sicilian Superfoods and the Mediterranean diet, Dr. Acquista explains why the Sicilian way of eating keeps you feeling full and satisfied while, at the same time, encouraging maximum weight loss without counting calories. For a weight loss plan (to lose up to 10 pounds in 2 weeks) as well as a maintenance program (to keep the weight off), read *The Mediterranean Prescription*.

Chapter One:
WHY SICILIANS DON'T GET FAT: The Sicilian Family Table

Among my many memories of growing up in Sicily, those of family meals are the most vivid and heartwarming. Italians love to eat, and they love to share food with family and friends. When I was a boy we went to my grandmother's house every Sunday for dinner, which was served in the early afternoon. There were always more than a dozen family members gathered around the table where we shared love and laughter along with our food. But even on weekdays my brother and I came home from school for lunch, and every night we ate dinner together as a family.

There was always an abundance of delicious food on the table. When it comes to food, *abbondanza* is the Sicilian byword. No one was ever on a diet, but—as far as I can remember—no one was fat either. For us, food was associated with pleasure and relaxation, not anxiety and guilt. We spent time at the table, eating multiple courses including *antipasti* (appetizers) and/or *insalati* (salads), *primi piatti* (first courses), *secondi* (main courses), and *contorni* (side dishes). But we rarely had *dolci* (sweet desserts). The truth is, by the time we finished all this, none of us had room for dessert.

So how could we eat so much and not worry about our weight? Part of the reason was certainly that the Sicilian lifestyle involved much more manual labor than most of us in the industrialized, digitalized Western world engage in today. These days people have to constantly run off to the gym (or around the park) to achieve the degree of activity we Sicilians engaged in as a natural part of daily life. More important, however, are the *kinds* of food we ate and the way those foods were prepared. A first course might be a small portion of pasta prepared with olive oil or a tomato-based sauce (never heavy cream), or a vegetable-based soup. The main course was usually some kind of fish (sometimes chicken, or, rarely, a small piece of grilled meat), and always two or three kinds of vegetables. The entrée was always broiled, grilled, or sautéed, not fried, and the vegetables were also broiled, boiled, or sautéed in olive oil.

If we did want dessert, it would be a handful of nuts, a piece of ripe fruit, berries, sometimes fresh, licorice-tasting fennel, or even—believe it or not—baked or grilled wild baby artichokes. And those are the very same foods we ate as snacks.

The foods that traditionally fill the Sicilian table and the way we ate in my boyhood home, and as I continue to eat today, promote both emotional and physical health. Most of us develop our lifelong eating habits as children, and the problem for many Americans is that those habits consist of eating fatty fried fast foods on the run, and rarely taking the time to discover the pleasures of preparing fresh foods and sitting down to enjoy them together as a family.

Without ever thinking about it, my family consumed the 7 Sicilian Superfoods at almost every meal. We ate that way because those were the foods available to us, and because the methods of preparation were handed down from one generation to the next. We now live in a world where the *abbondanza* I enjoyed as a boy is available to us year round wherever we live, and anyone can adopt the lifestyle I was lucky enough to have experienced naturally.

Chapter Two:
THE 7 SICILIAN SUPERFOODS

A growing amount of increasingly persuasive scientific and medical evidence indicates that the foods forming the basis of the Mediterranean diet promote weight loss and have significant benefits for every aspect of our health and well-being. Here they are, the 7 Superfoods, and just some of the studies attesting to their benefits.

Extra-Virgin Olive Oil

A recent study conducted at Oxford University in the UK found that consuming extra-virgin olive oil aids in the assimilation of vitamins and minerals and stimulates bone mineralization, thus preventing calcium loss, which leads to osteoporosis.

A separate Spanish case-control study compared the diets of 171 patients who had recently suffered a non-fatal heart attack with those of 171 non-heart attack patients of the same age. It found that those who consumed the most olive oil reduced their risk of heart attack by 82 percent.

Cruciferous Vegetables

When it comes to health benefits, not all vegetables are created equally. Cruciferous vegetables, which get their name from their "four-petaled flowers" that form the shape of a cross, include broccoli, broccoli rabe, cauliflower, brussels sprouts, bok choy, arugula, collards, kale, escarole, cabbage, radishes, turnips, watercress, mustard greens, and others.

A study conducted at the Roswell Park Cancer Center in Buffalo, New York, found that a number of isothiocyanates (ITCs), which are phytochemicals found in cruciferous vegetables, possess multiple anti-cancer properties that have been shown to be effective against both developing and developed cancer cells. In a study of more than 1,000 men conducted at the Fred Hutchinson Cancer Research Center in Seattle, WA, those eating 3 or more servings of vegetables a day lowered their risk of prostate cancer by 35 percent compared to those who ate fewer than 2 servings a day. Those who consumed just 3 or more servings of *cruciferous* vegetables each week had a 44 percent lower prostate cancer risk compared to those who ate less than 1 serving a week.

Tomatoes

A study published in *American Journal of Clinical Nutrition* found that patients with a type of polyp in the colon that is the precursor for most colorectal cancers had blood levels of lycopene (the pigment that gives tomatoes their bright red color) that were 35 percent *lower* than those of study subjects with no polyps. In their final analysis, only two things increased the likelihood of these colorectal polyps: low levels of lycopene in the blood (less than 70 micrograms per liter) and smoking. And the increase in risk was substantial: low levels of lycopene increased the risk by 230 percent and smoking increased the risk by 302 percent.

How do you avoid those low levels of lycopene? Tomatoes. Research conducted at Brigham and Women's Hospital in Boston, suggests that in addition to its inverse association with various cancers, a high dietary consumption of lycopene (tomatoes) may play a role in decreasing cardiovascular disease. The researchers tracked close to 40,000 middle-aged and older women who were free of both cardiovascular disease and cancer when the study began. During more than 7 years of follow-up, those who consumed 7 to 10 servings each week of lycopene-rich foods (tomato-based products including tomatoes, tomato juice, tomato sauce, and Sicilian pizza—which is different from the type of pizza we eat in the U.S.) were found to have a 29 percent lower risk of cardiovascular disease than women eating less than 1.5 servings of tomato products weekly.

In further support of this particular Superfood, the women in the study who ate more than 2 servings each week of oil-based tomato products, particularly tomato sauce and pizza, had an even better result—a 34 percent lower risk of cardiovascular disease.

More good news for the Mediterranean dieter eating the 7 Sicilian Superfoods: Olive oil enhances the absorption of lycopene. So eat them together!

Nuts

A 2002 study conducted by David Jenkins, M.D., and published in the journal *Circulation,* tested 27 men and women with high cholesterol levels over a period of 3 months and found that those who ate one handful of almonds a day lowered their bad (LDL) cholesterol by 4.4 percent, while those who ate two handfuls a day lowered their LDL levels by 9.4 percent.

A study conducted at the Harvard School of Public Health found that substituting the fat from 1 ounce of nuts for the equivalent energy (i.e. calories) from carbohydrates in an average diet was associated with a 30 percent reduction in coronary heart disease risk. The substitution of nut fat for saturated fat was associated with a 45 percent reduction in risk.

Berries

Among their rich supply of phytonutrients—nutrients found only in plants—blueberries contain a flavonoid (plant pigment) called kaempferol. Research calculating flavonoid intake in 66,940 women enrolled in the Nurses Health Study between 1984 and 2002 revealed that women whose diets provided the most kaempferol had a 40 percent reduction in risk of ovarian cancer, compared to women eating the least kaempferol-rich foods.

Research conducted in the Netherlands and published in the journal *BioFactors* showed that raspberries have almost 50 percent more antioxidant activity than strawberries, 3 times that of kiwis, and 10 times the antioxidant activity of tomatoes.

To explain the importance of these findings let me rely on some basic chemistry. When oxygen interacts with certain molecules in the body it can cause oxidative stress, which leads to the creation of what are called free radicals. Our bodies are made up of atoms and molecules, each of which contains one or more pairs of electrons. Free radicals are atoms or molecules that are missing one electron, which makes them unstable and causes them to try to complete their structure by "stealing" an electron from another, neighboring molecule. This prompts the molecule that's been "robbed" of its electron to do the same thing, causing a kind of domino effect that wreaks havoc on the molecular structure and stability of the body and causes inflammation on the cellular level. As a result, cells may function poorly, replicate abnormally (which gives rise to cancer), or they may die.

Antioxidants neutralize free radicals by donating one of their own electrons, ending the "electron-stealing" reaction. The antioxidant nutrients themselves don't become free radicals by donating an electron because they are stable in either form. They act as cellular stabilizers, helping to prevent cell and tissue damage that could lead to cellular damage, cancer, and other diseases.

Oxidative stress on the cellular level is the biological equivalent of what happens when a piece of metal is left out in the elements and rusts. It is aging itself. The antioxidants naturally occurring in berries and the other Sicilian Superfoods help to prevent that kind of deterioration from occurring in your body. Therefore, they are one of the many keys to living a long and healthy life.

Legumes (peas, lentils, string beans, lima beans, fava beans, chick peas, soy beans, red kidney beans, cannellini beans, pinto beans, beans of any kind, and others)

A study conducted at the Vanderbilt Epidemiology Center in Nashville, Tennessee, followed 64,227 middle aged Chinese women for more than 4 years and concluded that consumption of legumes was associated with a reduced rate of Type 2 diabetes.

In a study conducted at the Tulane School of Public Health and Epidemiology, 9,632 men and women who did not have cardiovascular disease were followed for a period of 19 years. At the end of that time, those who consumed legumes 4 times or more a week were found to have a 22 percent lower risk for coronary heart disease, and an 11 percent lower risk of cardiovascular disease than those who consumed legumes less than once a week. The researchers concluded that "increasing legume intake may be an important part of a dietary approach to the primary prevention of coronary heart disease in the general population."

Fresh Fish

A Greek study conducted by researchers at the University of Athens and published in the *American Journal of Clinical Nutrition* looked at more than 3,000 men and women ages 18 to 89 and found that eating at least 10 ounces of omega-3-rich fish each week improves the electrical properties of heart cells, protecting against fatal abnormal heart rhythms in people without evidence of other cardiovascular disease.

The International Study of Macro- and Micro-nutrients and Blood Pressure (known as INTERMAP) studied the effect of lifestyle and diet on hypertension in 4,680 men and women between the ages of 40 and 59 in Japan, China, the United States, and the United Kingdom. The researchers found that those who consumed greater amounts of omega-3 fatty acids (found in fish) had lower blood pressure than those who consumed less.

Most interestingly for our Sicily-centered Mediterranean diet, the researchers also found that omega-3s from nuts, seeds, and vegetable oils—such as walnuts and flaxseed—had just as much impact on blood pressure as omega-3s from fish. "With blood pressure, every millimeter counts. The effect of each nutrient is apparently small but together they can add up to a substantial impact on blood pressure. If you can reduce blood pressure a few millimeters from eating less salt, losing a few pounds, avoiding heavy drinking, eating more vegetables, whole grains and fruits (for their fiber, minerals, vegetable protein and other nutrients) and getting more omega-3 fatty acids, then you've made a big difference," said the lead author of the study, Hirotsugu Ueshima, MD, of Shiga University of Medical Science in Japan.

So, there you have it: Nothing could be more beneficial to your health than adopting a diet based on the 7 Sicilian Superfoods – alone or in combination. The gains are synergistic and the health benefits are undeniably powerful.

Chapter Three:
MYTHS AND MISCONCEPTIONS

There are many assumptions and misconceptions about fats—particularly about the association between fat consumption and weight gain. Most people believe that all fats are equal and that eating fat is the main reason people get fat.

Another widespread belief is that if we take vitamins and supplements we will be healthy, no matter what we eat, and that the health benefits of taking a pill or a capsule are equal to those we derive from consuming real foods.

There is growing scientific evidence that, contrary to popular belief, consuming olive oil does not lead to weight gain, and eating nuts does not make us fat. Additionally, the nutrients and phytochemicals we get from eating food are significantly more important for health than taking vitamins and supplements. And pasta—in and of itself—is not inherently "fattening." Rather, it's the quantities we eat and the types of sauces we tend to put on our pasta that add the pounds.

The Truth About Fat

Contrary to what many people believe, not all fats make you fat. All fats are not created equal, and the *kind of fat* you eat can have a meaningful effect on your overall health.

According to Katherine Zeratsky, a nutritionist at the Mayo Clinic,

"When choosing fats, olive oil is a healthy choice. Olive oil contains monounsaturated fat, a healthier type of fat that can lower your risk of heart disease by reducing the total and low-density lipoprotein (LDL, or "bad") cholesterol levels in your blood."

On the other hand, saturated and trans fats — such as butter, animal fats, tropical oils and partially hydrogenated oils — increase your risk of heart disease by increasing your total and LDL cholesterol levels.

But not all types of olive oil are equally healthy either. "Extra-virgin" or "virgin" olive oils are the least processed and, therefore, the most heart healthy. EVOO contains the highest levels of polyphenols, which are powerful antioxidants that can promote heart health.

Nuts Aren't Fattening Either!

Yes, nuts contain fat. But there are several studies to show that eating nuts will not cause you to gain weight, and may actually contribute to weight loss. Of course, if you're sitting at a bar or in a restaurant and your hand is constantly moving from nut bowl to mouth until the bowl is empty, and if you do this on a regular basis, you may very well gain weight—but again, it's how much you're eating that's to blame.

Researchers in the departments of nutrition and epidemiology at the School of Public Health, Loma Linda University, Loma Linda, CA, reported that people without any dietary restrictions who included nuts in their diet did not "have a higher body mass index or a tendency to gain weight" than those who did not eat nuts.

Why Not Just Take Supplements?

The number of vitamins and other supplements available to us seems to be growing by leaps and bounds—there's a health food store on almost every corner, a GNC branch in most malls, and many rows of shelf space devoted to them in every drugstore. But there is still little to no evidence that they actually work or that taking them can compensate for unhealthy eating.

For example, in a study funded by the National Cancer Institute, 20 participants were encouraged to eat 1 to 2 cups of cruciferous vegetables a day. After 3 weeks, the amount of oxidative stress in their bodies was measured. Then, after a 3week wash-out period, the study participants were told to take a multivitamin with fiber. Again, the oxidative stress was measured 3 weeks later.

The results? Oxidative stress in the subjects' bodies dropped 22% during the period when they were eating lots of cruciferous vegetables. But the change during the multivitamin segment was negligible (0.2%), according to the lead researcher Jay H. Fowke, PhD, an assistant professor and cancer epidemiologist for the Department of Medicine at Vanderbilt Medical Center in Nashville, Tennessee.

Chapter Four:

NATURAL WEIGHT LOSS THE SICILIAN WAY

The recipes here and those included in *The Mediterranean Prescription* promote significant weight loss and help break what may have become a lifetime habit of unhealthy eating. If you add an exercise component, you won't have to count calories or work out furiously to see results.

Because it is the southernmost tip of the Mediterranean, Sicily has the longest growing season and the greatest abundance of the foods that comprise the basis for the Mediterranean Diet. It is, in effect, the *ultimate* Mediterranean diet. In addition, the Sicilian lifestyle—again because of the warm climate—involves a significant amount of time outdoors engaging in physical activity as well as stress-reducing leisure time with friends and family, both of which work in conjunction with diet to enhance physical and emotional health.

I love to tell this story about my own wife, a former fashion model who is 5 feet 10 inches tall and weighs 130 pounds. She gained 60 pounds during her pregnancy, and four months after giving birth to our twins she returned to work having lost all the "baby weight." The people at the agency were amazed that she'd lost so much weight in such a short time and asked her how she did it. Her answer was simple: "My husband cooks for me." The recipes I made are the recipes included in this book. By following the Sicilian diet, she had naturally accomplished something most women struggle with—and she didn't have to count calories, hire a (personal) nutritionist (since I didn't charge for my services), or work out daily with a personal trainer.

How much weight you will lose when you start eating Mediterranean meals depends upon how much you weigh to begin with (in most cases, the heavier you are the more you will lose), how active you are, and how closely you adhere to the Mediterranean way. This diet will keep people feeling full and satisfied while eating foods that are tasty, simple to prepare, and encourage weight loss. There is an abundance of evidence to show that virtually any diet will work in the short term, but to *maintain* weight loss, your "diet" must be realistic, satisfying, and adaptable to a long-term change in lifestyle.

One important aspect of that change in lifestyle is to become more active. When I was growing up in Sicily being active was not something anyone had to think about much. We farmed; if we needed to go anywhere, we walked; my mother took care of the family's needs—cooking, cleaning, helping with the garden—without the aid of "labor-saving" devices. Now, for most of us, food comes from grocery stores (already peeled and chopped if you want it that way); public transportation and cars mean that we no longer have to use our feet to get around; and we have machines to do most of the cooking and cleaning for us. To lose weight and keep it off, daily exercise is a key component. We can do that naturally by walking more, climbing the stairs instead of taking the elevator, and playing with our kids. Gyms are everywhere if we need more discipline, as are exercise classes, and more. There are many ways to get moving without having to count reps or bench press heavy weights. And there is considerable medical evidence to show that people who are active are emotionally and physically healthier and leaner than those who are not.

Stick to two basic principles: First, make the 7 Sicilian Superfoods your dietary staples, and second, prepare them in the traditional Sicilian manner.

Try not to eat meat more than twice a week and don't eat more than 4 to 6 ounces at a time—accompanied by plenty of healthy vegetables.

As you lose weight, you'll feel better and you'll be able to increase your exercise level. In fact, the fitter you are, the more you'll *want* to move. Once physical activity becomes a part of your daily routine, you'll actually miss it when the routine is interrupted. Again, there is scientific evidence showing that the chemicals released in the brain and the body when we exercise contribute significantly to our sense of well-being for the rest of the day.

ANGELO'S FAMILY RECIPES

Antipasti (appetizers), *Primi Piatti* (First Courses), *Insalati* (Salads), and *Contorni* (Side Dishes)

MIXED SALAD

(This is quick, easy and delightful.)

Makes 4 servings

Ingredients

8 basil leaves, sliced

4 medium potatoes, boiled, peeled and cut into one inch cubes

8 plum tomatoes or 4 medium sized beef-steak tomatoes

1/2 cup mixed green and black olives (not ones from a can)

3 tablespoons washed capers

2 kirby cucumbers sliced

1 large onion sliced

4 tablespoons olive oil

Salt and pepper to taste

Preparation

Combine all of the above, add oil and gently mix.

CARROTS WITH LEMON AND MARSALA

Makes 4 servings

Ingredients

3 tablespoons olive oil

1 ½ pounds carrots, peeled, quartered, and cut into 2-inch-long strips

1/2 cup marsala wine

2 tablespoons flat-leaf parsley, finely chopped

1 teaspoon freshly squeezed lemon juice

Salt and pepper to taste

Preparation

Set a pan over medium heat. When hot, add olive oil and carrots. Cook, stirring frequently, for 4 to 6 minutes. Season with salt and pepper and add marsala wine. Cover the pan and cook for 12 minutes. When fork tender, add parsley and lemon juice and serve.

ESCAROLE AND BEANS

Makes 6 servings

Ingredients

2 large bunches of escarole

1/2 cup olive oil

1 clove garlic, minced

4 cups of cooked or canned cannellini beans

2 cups of water

Salt and pepper to taste

Preparation

Remove tough outer leaves from escarole and discard. Remove remaining leaves from root end and wash thoroughly. Bring 3 inches of water to a boil in a large pot and add escarole. Boil over high heat for 5 minutes. Drain and cool escarole in ice water, then dry on paper towels. Sauté olive oil and garlic in a large sauté pan over medium to low heat for 1 minute. Stir in beans and add escarole, 2 cups water, and salt and pepper to taste. Lower heat, cook for 5 minutes, and serve hot.

BROCCOLI RABE AND FAVA BEANS

Makes 4 servings

Ingredients

2 bunches broccoli rabe, washed a..

large leaves

1 pound shelled fava beans

4 cloves crushed garlic

3 tablespoons olive oil

1 tablespoon salt

1/2 teaspoon pepper

Preparation

In a large pot bring 3 quarts of water to a boil. Add salt and broccoli rabe. Let it boil for one additional minute. Remove the broccoli rabe, and place it in a large serving bowl along with 1/2 cup of the water. Keep near stove and cover to keep it warm. In the same water add fava beans and garlic, bring to a boil, then lower heat, cover and let simmer for approximately 20 minutes. Drain fava beans from water and combine with broccoli rabe. Drizzle with oil, add pepper and serve hot.

AND POTATO SALAD

vings

ents

s good quality mackerel filets, drained of their oil

ups chopped hearts of romaine

2 plum tomatoes seeded and chopped

20 black cured olives

2 yukon gold potatoes, boiled and diced

1/2 cup diced celery

1/2 sweet medium onion, sliced

4 tablespoons olive oil

2 tablespoons white wine vinegar

1 tablespoon capers

1 teaspoon salt

1 tablespoon ground black pepper

Preparation

In a large bowl combine romaine, tomatoes, olives, capers, potatoes, onion, celery and mackerel. In a separate small bowl combine and mix oil, vinegar, salt, and pepper. Pour into larger bowl. Mix gently and serve.

BEET AND WATERCRESS SALAD

Makes 4 servings

Ingredients

6 medium sized beets, washed

1 bunch watercress, washed and cut in half

1/2 cup lightly toasted walnuts

Juice of 1 lemon

3 tablespoons olive oil

2 tablespoons water

1 teaspoon salt

1 teaspoon pepper

Preparation

Preheat oven to 425°F. Place washed beets in a baking pan. Add water, cover with aluminum foil and place in oven for 50 to 60 minutes, until fork tender. Remove from oven, peel skin off the beets, cut into bite-size pieces, and place in a salad bowl. Add watercress, oil, lemon juice, salt and pepper. Mix well. Place on individual serving plates and sprinkle with walnuts.

CHILLED CRUNCHY SALAD

(This is a great salad that is quick and easy. You may add flaked canned tuna and convert this salad to a meal. In Sicily, my mother would add baby green cantaloupe which has a more intense flavor than cucumbers.)

Makes 4 servings

Ingredients

1 bunch celery, sliced with tough outer stalks removed

1 bunch radishes, trimmed, washed and sliced

3 kirby cucumbers, sliced

1 bulb of fennel sliced, tough outer husk removed

Juice of 1 1/2 lemons

3 tablespoons olive oil

1 teaspoon salt

1 teaspoon pepper

Preparation

In a salad bowl combine celery, radishes, cucumbers and fennel. Refrigerate for 1/2 hour to 1 hour. Before serving, mix well with oil, lemon juice, salt, and pepper.

FENNEL SALAD

(This is a wonderful refreshing salad that we used to serve in Sicily before or while we ate our appetizers. Packs a tremendous amount of fiber that will give you a sense of satiety.)

Makes 4 servings

Ingredients

4 bulbs of fennel with green stems trimmed

4 tablespoons extra virgin olive oil

Juice of 1 lemon

1 teaspoon salt

1 teaspoon pepper

Preparation

Remove tough outer husk from fennel and discard. Thinly slice the fennel, about 1/8 inch thick, and place in a salad bowl. Cover with plastic wrap and refrigerate. When ready to serve, add olive oil, salt, pepper, and lemon juice. Mix well.

FENNEL AND *ORANGE* SALAD

Makes 4 servings

Ingredients

4 bulbs of fennel with green stems removed

4 tablespoons of extra virgin olive oil

1 orange, quartered and cut into ¼-inch slices

1 tablespoon freshly squeezed lemon juice

1 teaspoon salt

1 teaspoon pepper

Preparation

Prepare fennel as in the previous fennel salad, removing the tough, outer husk and slicing into thin 1/8 inch thick strips. Add sliced orange and refrigerate. When ready to eat, combine salt, pepper, olive oil, and lemon juice. Mix well and serve.

TOMATO AND ANCHOVY SALAD

Makes 4 servings

Ingredients

20 pitted, oil cured olives

10 anchovy filets

1 tablespoon drained capers

2 cups cherry tomatoes cut in half

1 sweet medium onion, sliced

3 tablespoons olive oil

Salt and pepper to taste

Preparation

Combine olives, anchovy filets, capers, onions, and tomatoes. Mix with oil, add salt and pepper, and serve.

TUNA CARPACCIO ANTIPASTO

Serves 4

Ingredients

1/4 pound sushi-grade tuna

2 teaspoons lemon juice

2 tablespoons orange juice

2 tablespoons olive oil

Kosher salt

Fresh ground black pepper

Preparation

Cut the tuna in 4 equal pieces. Place 1 piece at a time between 2 pieces of plastic wrap and gently pound the tuna to desired thickness. Peel off the plastic and place tuna on a plate. Sprinkle it with salt and pepper. Mix the lemon and orange juice together, sprinkle tuna with juice mixture. Drizzle with olive oil, and serve.

BOILED OCTOPUS ANTIPASTO

Makes 4 servings

Ingredients

4 pounds octopus

2 lemons

2 tablespoons salt

Preparation

Bring a large pot of salted water to boil. Use enough water to fully cover the octopus. Gently immerse the tentacles of the octopus into boiling water 3 times while holding it by its head. Then drop the entire octopus in the water. Cook for 20 to 40 minutes. Taste one of the tentacles to check for tenderness. May need to cook for 5 to 10 minutes longer. Drain from water, cut into 1-inch pieces, place on a serving platter, and squeeze lemon juice on top. Serve hot or cold.

TUNA AND CANELLINI BEAN BRUSCHETTA

Serves 6-8

Ingredients

1 12-ounce can of drained cannellini beans

2 6-ounce cans of tuna, preferably Progresso or Genoa canned tuna, drained of its oil

3 finely minced garlic cloves, sautéed

1 teaspoon finely chopped sage or thyme (one or the other, not both)

Bread

4 tablespoons extra virgin olive oil

Salt and pepper to taste

Preparation

Place beans and tuna in a bowl and mash with a fork. Sprinkle with oil, sage or thyme, salt and pepper. Serve on toasted bread with a little drizzle of oil on top.

STRING BEANS WITH ALMONDS AND CHEESE

Serves 4

Ingredients

1 pound trimmed string beans

3 tablespoons toasted plain bread crumbs

3 tablespoons grated Pecorino Romano cheese (or you can substitute parmeggiano)

3 tablespoons sliced toasted almonds

2 tablespoons olive oil

1 tablespoon salt

Preparation

In a pot of salted, boiling water, cook the string beans until tender (about 4 minutes) and drain. Place beans in a sauté pan, drizzle with oil, turn off heat and mix with almonds, breadcrumbs, and cheese. Stir to coat the beans and serve.

Secondi (Main Courses)

PASTA WITH GRILLED (NOT FRIED) EGGPLANT AND TOMATO SAUCE

Makes 4 to 6 servings

Ingredients

1 ½ pounds eggplant, cut into 1/2 inch cubes

1 medium onion, chopped

4 cloves garlic, crushed

1 24-ounce can Italian crushed tomatoes

1 tablespoon tomato paste

1 pound penne or ziti pasta, cooked according to package directions

2 tablespoons chopped basil

Freshly grated pecorino cheese

12 tablespoons olive oil

Salt and pepper to taste

Preparation

Arrange the eggplant in a single layer in a large baking pan. Drizzle with 4 tablespoons of olive oil. Season with salt and pepper to taste and broil 8 inches from heat source for 5 to 7 minutes, until lightly golden on all sides. Remove pan and set aside.

Heat another 4 tablespoons of the oil in a large sauté pan. Add the onion and garlic and sauté until the onions are translucent. Remove the garlic, add the tomato paste, tomatoes and grilled eggplant, and bring sauce to a boil. Lower heat and simmer for 15 minutes.

Add well-drained, cooked ziti or penne to pan with eggplant and sauce, and cook together, stirring, for one minute. Remove from heat and sprinkle with the remaining 4 tablespoons of olive oil, the pecorino cheese, and basil. Serve at once.

SPAGHETTINI WITH BROCCOLI

Makes 4 servings

Ingredients

1 pound broccoli, cut into florets

1 pound spaghettini

4 cloves garlic, finely chopped

Freshly grated pecorino cheese

10 tablespoons olive oil

Salt and pepper to taste

Preparation

Cook the broccoli in 4 quarts of boiling salted water for 3 to 4 minutes, until crisp-tender. Do not drain. Remove the broccoli with a slotted spoon and rinse under cold running water to stop the cooking. Pat it dry and set aside. Add the spaghettini to the broccoli water and cook according to package directions.

While the pasta cooks, heat 6 tablespoons of olive oil in a large sauté pan. Add the garlic and broccoli and sauté for 1 minute. Drain the cooked spaghettini reserving 2 ladles of the water. Add the pasta and reserved cooking water to the broccoli and cook, while stirring, for 1 minute. Remove from the heat, add the remaining 4 tablespoons of oil, and add a generous amount of pecorino cheese. Season with salt and pepper to taste, and serve.

LINGUINI WITH SWORDFISH

(Even people who don't like swordfish love this recipe.)

Makes 6 servings

Ingredients

1½ pounds skinless and boneless swordfish steaks, cut into 1-inch cubes

1 pound linguini, cooked al dente according to package directions

1/3 cup white wine

1 medium onion, chopped

1 24-ounce can whole peeled Italian plum tomatoes crushed with your hands

1 tablespoon tomato paste

1/2 cup water

1/2 cup fresh, roughly chopped mint

10 tablespoons olive oil

Salt and pepper to taste

Preparation

Season the swordfish on all sides with salt and pepper. Heat a sauté pan over medium heat. Add 6 tablespoons of the olive oil and the swordfish. Sauté the fish, turning to cook each side for 2 minutes (a total of 4 minutes). Add the wine, turn the heat to high, and cook 1 minute more. Remove the fish from the pan with a slotted spoon and set aside. Add the onion and a pinch of salt to the pan and sauté until translucent. Add the tomatoes, tomato paste, 1 teaspoon of salt, and the water, and simmer for 10 minutes. Return the swordfish to the pan and cook for 4 minutes. Add mint and stir into sauce. Add the cooked and drained linguini to the sauce and cook for 1 more minute. Sprinkle with the remaining 4 tablespoons of olive oil. Stir and serve immediately.

TUNA WITH LEMON AND ORANGE SAUCE

Makes 4 servings

Ingredients

4 (4-to-6-ounce) tuna steaks, cut 1-inch thick

Juice of 2 oranges and the zest of 1 orange

Juice and zest of 2 small lemons

1/4 cup marsala wine

2 tablespoons flat-leaf parsley, finely chopped

4 tablespoons olive oil

Salt and pepper to taste

Preparation

Season tuna with salt and pepper. Heat olive oil in a large sauté pan. Add seasoned tuna steaks and cook over medium heat for 1 to 2 minutes on each side. Remove tuna from pan and keep warm in a 175 degree oven. Add orange juice, lemon juice, and marsala to the pan and raise heat to high. Reduce the mixture by 1/4 and add orange zest and lemon zest. Season the sauce with salt and pepper to taste, pour over the tuna steaks, sprinkle with parsley, and serve.

BAKED SOLE FILET

Makes 4 servings

Ingredients

4 sole filets (approximately six ounces each)

1/4 cup flavored bread crumbs

2 tablespoons finely chopped parsley

1/2 teaspoon crushed dry thyme

4 lemon wedges

2 tablespoons olive oil

1 teaspoon salt

1 teaspoon black ground pepper

Preparation

Preheat oven to 450°F. Place fish filets in oiled baking pan. Brush filets with 2 tablespoons of oil, sprinkle with salt and pepper. Combine bread crumbs, parsley, and thyme in bowl and mix. Sprinkle bread crumb mixture over top of fish and place pan in oven for 10 minutes. Remove fish from oven, drizzle with remaining olive oil, and serve with lemon wedges.

TROUT IN WINE

Makes 4 servings

Ingredients

4 whole trout heads, scaled and cleaned

1 1/2 cups of red wine

1 cup white wine vinegar

1 cup water

4 sprigs thyme

4 bay leaves

8 whole cloves

1 carrot, sliced

Rind of 1 lemon

2 tablespoons chopped parsley

1 tablespoon black pepper corns

1 medium onion, sliced

3 tablespoons olive oil

Salt and pepper to taste, plus 1 teaspoon salt

Preparation

In a roasting pan place trout in a single layer. Sprinkle with salt and pepper on both sides. Bring wine vinegar to a boil and pour over the trout. Let marinate for 30 minutes. Remove from pan and place fish in a large skillet. Discard vinegar.

In a saucepan combine lemon rind, cloves, wine, carrot, onion, parsley, thyme, peppercorns, bay leaves, and water. Bring to a boil.

Add boiling mixture to skillet, cover and slowly simmer for 15 to 20 minutes. Carefully remove fish from skillet and arrange in a large serving dish. Reduce the remaining liquid to 1/3 of a cup, strain liquid, and pour over fish. Sprinkle with olive oil and serve.

BAKED BRANZINO (SEA BASS)

Makes 4 servings

Ingredients

2 branzino (2 pounds each), scaled, cleaned and dried

4 sprigs fresh rosemary

2 tablespoons olive oil

4 lemon slices

Sauce:

2 tablespoons olive oil

1 tablespoon lemon juice

4 tablespoons water

2 fresh bay leaves

2 garlic cloves, crushed

2 teaspoons capers

2 teaspoons salt

Black pepper

Preparation

Place two sprigs of rosemary and 2 lemon slices in cavity of each fish. Brush fish on both sides with olive oil, place in baking pan and broil each side for 5 minutes.

Sauce:

In a food processor, place garlic, salt, pepper, water, capers, lemon juice, oil, rosemary, and bay leaves. Liquidize until smooth. Spoon liquid over fish and serve.

TUNA IN GARLIC AND VINEGAR

Makes 4-6 servings

Ingredients

2 pounds tuna slices 1/2 inch thick

3 garlic cloves, sliced

4 tablespoons mint, chopped

1/2 cup white wine vinegar

4 tablespoons olive oil

Salt and pepper

Preparation

Sauté tuna slices in hot olive oil 30 seconds on each side. Remove tuna from pan. In the remaining oil, add garlic. When garlic is golden, add vinegar. Bring to boil, add mint, salt, and pepper to taste, pour on top of tuna. Refrigerate and serve cold.

PESTO ALLA TRAPANESE

Makes 4 servings

Ingredients

1 pound spaghetti

2 cups cherry tomatoes

3 garlic cloves

1 bunch or 2 cups of basil

1/2 cup almonds

2/3 cup olive oil, plus 3 tablespoons

1/2 cup grated parmeggiano cheese

1 teaspoon salt

1/2 teaspoons red pepper flakes

Preparation

In a large pot of salted boiling water add spaghetti. In a sauté pan on medium heat gently toast almonds. Place almonds in a food processor along with garlic, and mix for 30 seconds. Add basil, salt, pepper flakes, and tomatoes, and blend for another 30 seconds while slowly adding olive oil. Add cheese and blend for another 5 seconds. Place pesto in a large pan on medium heat. Add well-drained spaghetti and mix thoroughly for 20 seconds. Sprinkle with remaining oil and serve.

GROUPER IN TOMATO OLIVE AND CAPER SAUCE

Makes 4-6 servings

Ingredients

2 pounds grouper filet cut into 2-inch cubes

1/2 cup flour (for dredging fish)

1 large onion, thinly sliced

3 celery stalks, hearts with leaves, finely chopped

3 tablespoons of capers in brine (but not the brine itself)

1 cup pitted Sicilian green olives, cut in half

1 large can peeled plum tomatoes, crushed by hand

2 cups water

10 leaves of basil, sliced

1/2 cup olive oil plus 2 tablespoons

1 teaspoon red pepper flakes

1 tablespoon salt

Preparation

Salt the fish and dredge in flour. Add oil to hot pan and sauté fish for 1 1/2 minutes.

Turn and sauté for another 1/2 minute. Remove fish from pan and place on a platter. To the remaining oil, add onion, garlic, celery, 1/2 teaspoon salt, and pepper flakes. Cook for 2-3 minutes, stirring continuously. Add olives and capers and let cook for another minute or two.

Pour in the tomatoes and 2 cups of water, basil, and 1/2 teaspoon salt, bring to a boil, lower heat to medium and cook for 5 to 7 minutes, keeping the pan covered, and occasionally shaking it. Add fish in single layer along with its juices, simmer for another 7-10 minutes, again shaking the pan occasionally. Add remaining olive oil and serve.

BROILED COD FISH WITH CAPER SAUCE

Makes 4 servings

Ingredients

4 (6-ounce) cod steaks

6 tablespoons olive oil

2 tablespoons capers, drained

Juice of 2 lemons

2 tablespoons flat-leaf parsley, chopped

Salt and pepper to taste

Preparation

Preheat the broiler. Brush both sides of the cod with 2 tablespoons of olive oil. Season both sides with salt and pepper. Broil the cod about 7 to 8 inches from the heat source for 5 minutes on each side. In a small saucepan, heat the remaining 4 tablespoons of oil, the capers, and the lemon juice for 1 minute. Remove from heat, add parsley, and stir. Pour over the cod steaks and serve.

SPAGHETTI WITH SEA URCHINS

Makes 4 servings

Ingredients

1 pound spaghetti

2 boxes raw sea urchins (these can be purchased at specialty fish stores)

1/2 cup chopped parsley

1/3 cup olive oil

8 cloves of garlic sliced

Rind of 1 lemon

1 teaspoon red pepper flakes

Salt

Preparation

In a salted pot of boiling water, add spaghetti. In a large, hot frying pan, add 1/2 of the oil, red pepper flakes, and garlic. Sauté for 1 minute. Add two ladles of pasta water to frying pan. Two minutes before pasta is cooked, drain, and add to frying pan. Cook for 1 minute on medium heat, stir in parsley and lemon zest, and remove from heat. Add remaining olive oil, gently stir in sea urchins, and serve.

ABOUT ANGELO

Having received his medical degree from New York University School of Medicine, Dr. Angelo Acquista is board certified in internal medicine, pulmonary medicine, and tropical diseases. He is a clinical instructor in medicine at New York University Medical Center and managing director of the Pulmonary Critical Care Group LLC in Manhattan.

New York Mayor Rudy Giuliani named Dr. Acquista to the position of medical director for the New York City Office of Emergency Management. Dr. Acquista also served on the Mayor's Task Force on Bioterrorism. He is the author of the *New York Times* bestseller *The Survival Guide.*

Throughout his medical career, Dr. Acquista has been aware of and concerned about the many ways in which obesity and being overweight negatively affect health and longevity and has tried to help his patients lose weight and eat healthier. His book, *The Mediterranean Prescription* (Ballantine 2006), has sold more than 40,000 copies in hardcover and continues to sell several hundred copies every week. *Mediterranean Meals* picks up where *The Mediterranean Prescription* leaves off: bringing the scientific research up to date, providing 25 brand new, delicious, healthy recipes, and focusing specifically on the proven "Superfoods" that Dr. Acquista grew up eating in his native Sicily.

For more information about Dr. Acquista, about the Mediterranean lifestyle, and for even more recipes, please visit his website, www.mediterraneanrx.com or follow him on twitter: @DrAcquista.

48688735R00035

Made in the USA
Lexington, KY
11 January 2016